TWO WING

Mark McHugh-Pratt

Jock Stein

Typeset in 11.5pt Baskerville Old Face

and published in 2012 by

The Handsel Press
at 35 Dunbar Rd, Haddington EH41 3PJ

jstein@handselpress.org.uk

Cover design and printing by
West Port Print & Design Ltd, St Andrews (01334 477135)

Illustrations by Margaret Stein

British Library Cataloguing in Publication Data:
A catalogue record for this publication
is available from the British Library

ISBN   978-1-871828-73-3

A Short Introduction

Verse often has rhyme as well as rhythm; some say it frees the writer to let content make its own impact, others find it too constricting. These days, rhyme – apart from rap – has largely fallen out of fashion. Jock typically uses it, while Mark generally uses free verse with the occasional rhyme.

Whatever the style, poetry addresses particular situations, within and beyond the experience of the writers, in the hope that the rhythm and the content of the poem will communicate. If 'no man is an island', then our hope is that something deeper and more lasting than mere island-hopping will take place as you read these very different poems.

The title comes from the first poem, which celebrates the idea of balance, not as an armchair philosopher who might hope to take 'a balanced view' of human affairs, but as a marvel and mystery of creation, something we discover more and more as we reflect on the world of nature, and wonder at the privilege of being human in this extraordinary world. After we had chosen it, we discovered it expressed in a different context in the writings of the Sufi poet and mystic Mevlana Rumi, 'God turns you from one feeling to another and teaches by means of opposites, so that you will have *two wings to fly*, not one.' André Gide later expressed the thought in another way: 'L'étincelle de la vie ne saurait jaillir qu'entre deux pôles contraires.'

These poems for the most part reflect a personal faith. Mark and Jock come from different Christian traditions, but share an enthusiasm for God, for life, and for the journey of faith.

Butterfly Bush

Elegant cloud of blossoms
pouring energy, colour, scent;
a glorious bush of purple spikes
beckoning insects: 'Flutter by
and perch a longish while
with biological intent.'

The table now is spread:
soon comes a butterfly
and sets its folded wings
by nectar-laden blooms.
What drives this tiny brain
to such great energy?
What motivates this fragile thing
to dart with zig zag zooms
from here to there and back?
How flowers amazing synergy
'tween plant and insect?
Whence comes this daylight zest
and instinct that this bush
is home – a willing host
for all these flying visitors
who come for active rest,
recreation on a purple perch,
mind and tongue engrossed
in silent concentration?

Who designed such scenes
for tiny garden passengers –
or should I say, 'These things
that fascinate our human thoughts
are just within our genes?'

Maybe the truth requires to fly
on two well balanced wings.

JS July 2009

The Burn

The burn flows quieter now;
Detritus lies on rock and bank,
torn from its place by winter rains
when raging from its height, the burn
brought terror and disaster,
as the spent rubbish cast away
by fools and careless youth
threatened to block the passage of its life.

In its wild winter rush,
it caught up all the rubbish it could find,
and bore it onward, 'til it found
a tree, wind-torn from its safe rooting
blocking its path.
And then the rubbish, filling out the holes
and gaps within the branches
sought to deny it passage totally.

And so it would have died,
or flooded over bank and human pathway,
had not a push from some external force
begun to clear the rubbish from the tree.
And now it seems that all this never happened;
no storm, no danger and no flood.
But quietly it chatters on its way,
its waters clear, its passage sure.

MMP February 1998

2

Birthday Party

Thérèse: little known by the guest
who comes for party dressed,
but known far more by Mark
with whom she shares her life
and dislike of the dark
damp winter view of Fife
across the Forth. Come Spring,
when birds and all horizons sing.

JS

The Guardians

The eyes of Fife are watchful now,
now that the night has fallen,
and the train from London, softly past Dunbar,
bears aching cargo on to Waverley.
The Forth lights wink and warn
but there is none to heed their message
and the long burden of the day
is yielded to the slumber of the night.

MMP 24 Sep 2009

Scent from Patmos

1

Patmos: island cabin of my present past,
memory-scented, full of windows
opening one by one upon the life of Christ:
a mystery which wafts like incense to
and from my mind, and joins
each praying friend who knows my fate
and keeps me minded; gentle warriors
who blow back the smoke of Caesar
smothering me with lies, to kill my senses
and my prophecy. Scent of sea, my prison,
every tide a jailer teasing me upon the ebb
with invitation false, and telling me again
upon the flow that Caesar rules. I see
the shore, I smell the wind that moves so free
across that sea, while I must stop and swing
a censor with my prayers: so dream I will.

2

Scent of time, as by the Word God brought to be
all things, and set a stage for human history:
until God scented time was right for logic
to reshape itself within a womb, one womb for all.

3

Scent of wine, and wonder: thirty gallon jars
poured out their secret, and the wedding feast
resumed its course: a sign of joy restored,
a sign of glory and of God. We trusted him.

4

Scent of mystery: Nicodemus came with mindset
troubled to the Lord by night; he heard the word
of water and of Spirit, only way to clean the hearts
and nostrils that we use to sniff the cosmos.

5

Scent of earth: as Jesus took the clay and mixed it
into mud, and packed blind eyes which peered
and peered again, until they saw the one true light
which shines, and shines until full day has come.

6

Scent of power: this prophet healed the paralysed
and lame, testing Roman strength and Jewish wisdom;
breaking human limits, leaving one or two deep hints
of God's own fragrant secret – kingdom life.

7

Scent of death in Martha's worried nose which turned
to life when brother Lazarus came from darkness.
and we knew that cemeteries could hold us down
no longer. Resurrection rules, and death is dead.

8

Scent of oil which Mary poured on Jesus' feet
and stroked them with her hair for love. And
scent of dung when Judas whinged about its price
and shut the magic window of the word of grace.

9

Scent of blood as Roman scourges tore his flesh,
and flies and dirt devoured the fragrant gift of God
and followed him to death; while I could smell
the weight of sin that lay on him who carried it for all.

10

Scent of fish, cooking now upon a beach-laid fire
and blending with the voice of one alive
who called, "My children, come for breakfast!"
Fish, and bread, and all of us transformed.

11

Scent of holy motherhood, as Mary lived with me,
remembered, shared her heart and memories
in Ephesus; the place where God commanded me
to pitch my tent and serve his revelation.

12

Now I write my vision, shape my scents, unfold
my ears on purpose for this message to the seven:
Letters crafted from the furnishings of heaven –
stars, and sword, and waterfalls – pictures
ploughed into the soil of pagan cities,
to bear harvest in my time, and times to come.
Seven lampstands and their oil lit up for God.
What smoke? The pure, sweet incense of a faithful
company? The acrid stench of compromise?
The half-rich, tired scent of love gone cool?
My nose, my ear, my eye lie dead before you.
Lift me, give me life in every sense
that I may breathe and smell the air of heaven,
cross the sea that pounds me into exile,
taste the word that reconnects me to
my future; post these letters to your people.

*JS   Based on John's Gospel and the book of Revelation,
written during a visit to the locations of the Seven Churches,
to which the apostle addressed chapters 2 and 3 of the book.*

Who am I?

Who am I? I am a lamp and a mirror,
a beam in the darkness and also that darkness.
I overcome all, and am overcome by all.
Give me all that I need, and I shall be empty,
deprive me of all, and my cup will run with good.

Who am I? The hope and despair of my father,
the delight and repugnance of my mother,
the incomprehension of my brothers,
the light and dullness in the eyes of my beloved.

I am the sum of all my hopes and fears,
the knotty puzzle all my questions fail to solve,
the maze in which I lose my way;
and yet I fear lest day should end
before my life awareness send.

I am myself.

MMP

This Tender Spark

This tender spark
of life: your gift,
flesh with your mark
O God, to lift
heart, spirit, mind.
A love to find.

*JS Written for the baptism of Rachel Joanna Maxwell,
born 4 Feb 1991*

Will Homan's Lectern

Who knows this tree of oak
which years and years ago
to grace a church was felled?
But now the furnishings
are scattered, but not lost,
for Will, by generosity compelled,
(a craftsman we *do* know)
has made this lectern. Art,
which common gifts excelled
has crossed the boundaries
of language, land and sea,
fraternity to weld.

JS

Inward Journey

The axe, first, taken to the root,
blow after blow till the long slow fall
to supplication, upon God's mercy.

Mute, I am stripped, dismembered, severed
of all that gives me life,
cut and broken till the heart of me
is opened, till the backbone of my life
is evident.

There, hidden in the grain and
deeply penetrated through the wood,
yielding its fragrance to the world,
and later, shaped to show its
royal form and fashion, with
the message that it brings,
is God.

MMP

Columba's Oak

Columba saw me, fresh-earthed in the eastern soil,
an oak of Derry minding him of Ireland,
with burnished leaves of gold far spreading,
balanced by rootstems proudly reaching
unseen beneath the unresponsive earth.
Not berried like the other saplings, soon to bare
beseeching branches to a pagan sky.
He blessed me here and left me as a token,
a meeting place for those touched by his love.

I sense him now, and see his other soulmates
weeping around that figure 'fore the altar
westward for ever, on Iona's shore.

*MMP, written during a creative writing
workshop at Craigencalt*

Northwards

I will accompany the sun in its rising,
Dressed in gold threads among the sheltering clouds,
Its autumn glory hidden in the hill
A psalm of splendour and a hymnal light.

So will my burning rock rise with the day
and keep me company although I see it not;
surely this place is meant to be a haven
offering solitude and vision,
sweet companionship and union
where I may rest and safely be.

But it is shelter, not arrival;
tortured by bonds that tie me to the land,
hounded by hum and chastened by the noise of numbers
here, I drew down power to move, set forth,
abandon the constructed sense of self
and travel rudderless upon the Sea of Love.

After another life of weary travel, blessing too,
I landed broken but whole upon a rocky shore,
laboured to build again a place of shelter
quiet amidst the thunder of the waves
I sang my soundless song of celebration
naked upon the island shore.

And as I sing my song of scouring joy
examening the voyage I have made
I mind the passions of the past
that draw me to their drowsy cemeteries.
But binding ties are soluble in brine
and break if not continually renewed.

Quickly I open up another door
set in the inland wall of my poor cott
and through it view the mountains tall and bare
where lies my path; not back, not here
but on the stony pathway; through the
ice and snow, beyond the howling dark,
there lies my refuge.

*MMP   A response to a workshop based on 'A Song
among the Stones' by Kenneth Steven, 1 October 2011*

The Invitation

Yes, it has been long, this journey,
and a struggle from the first.
I did not expect understanding
but received love and care as well
which warmed and gratified my heart.
Now here I stand, watching my cousin
at his work, turning the curious
and those who mocked into
expectant people.
Now comes my turn to love and care
and tell much more than I am able;
I have left father for Father,
seen for Unseen,
safety for prayerful Uncertainty.
Soon as I move down from this gentle hill
he'll recognise me and will speak the words
which will unveil me.
What I long for most is company –
though it will bring both joy and pain.
Will you come with me ?   *MMP*

Glastonbury

What do you expect in Glastonbury?
Merlin, magic or a quieter past
spoken in ruined abbey and piled stone
rough to touch and tongue?
I tried to taste the past in the Abbey kitchen
but the bare stone made me fast
on the seats laid out for tourist tasters,
roast and herb unsung.
Instead I climbed the twisting hill
and found the summit Tor at last,
seeing, feeling Avalon's stories
breathed into a lung
of myth and memory. Now to home
skies, working grey and overcast,
I travel, thankful, fed in spirit
and around my heart hope hung.

JS, written during a CARM retreat, July 2011

Incarnation

Soaring space
vanishes into metaphor;
high and low span
this divine care plan,
texted in psalm,
shaped in Mary's womb:
pride unhorsed,
humility endorsed,
all open before
the lightning flash of God
who earths his hero
at ground zero.

JS Based on Psalm 138 verse 6

Multum in Parvo

I have seen
The island of the holy.
I have heard
seals sing, ducks declare and birds babble
psalms and gossip to their maker.

I have been
to the shore's edge, and watched
the curious interplay of sea and land and air
upon the island of the holy.

I have observed
the tourists talk of bread and milk and cornflakes,
Of the tides and stones and saints
in the island of the holy.

I have believed that here, as elsewhere
everyday and holy day
sea and land and air
Island and Mainland
Saints and Sinners
Self and Others
God
are One.

MMP March 2007

Vincent Vanquished

Plums – how long have I sought them,
plucked them, tasted them,
felt their richness on my tongue,
my mind in torment calmed and satisfied
until their succulence had disappeared.

A life ago I saw their parents on a tree,
promising much at harvest time.
Captured on canvas and within my heart,
they gave me hope for times to come.

Yet, though I turned my face up to the sky,
aping the flowers that flourish so,
the colours , brightened by its glare
burned like a brand within my brain.

I turned away, blackened the windows
of my soul and cowered within;
Paul, whom I loved but could not bear,
and Dr Gachet, with his own distress,
pulled down his shutters too.

So I went out again to search
and searched in vain
for all that promised fruit.

But finding naught but ripened corn
with carrion circling for my blood,
I tried to put a bullet in my heart;
harvest of hope
lost.

MMP December 2010

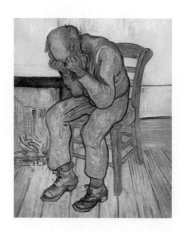

Vision

I lift up my head.
On the windowsill
lie articles of daily beauty –
photographs, small vases of flowers,
    books;
I drink.

> I lift up my head.
> There, there is green –
> of the short space of lawn, of the hedge,
> of the finches mingled with brown and gold
> eager for food from the feeders, seed
> for themselves and for their young.
> I drink.

> > I lift up my head.
> > Green – green again,
> > the green of the burgeoning wheat
> > ruffled by gusts of wind
> > stretching down, down to the hedge below
> > promising both kinds of bread
> > for farmer and family.
> > I eat.

> > > I lift up my head.
> > > Hardly heard and scarcely seen
> > > the toylike vehicles proceed on rail and road
> > > feeding the mouths of industry and leisure
> > > burning the stored goodness of the earth.
> > > I choke.

I lift up my head.
And there, beyond the sloping fields
and pantiled roofs
the breakers fall on sand and rock.
fringing a feast for eye and soul.
And on that wide expanse
bordered by villages and towns beyond
vessels of every size and shape
go quietly about their business.
I take it in.

 I lift up my head.
 The mobile heavens harbour
 space for no static creature.
 All there is movement,
 whether the constant morphing of the clouds
 or playful passion of the birds,
 joyful display of kite and child
 trying to tame the gusty wild,
 or the intrusive power of metal wings
 being the least of airborne things.
 I enter in.

  Where is the furthest of this visual tour
  of human being and of nature's power?
  Past all the reach of eye and word
  past all the strength that worlds afford
  past all that's music in the world
  there is a Silence spread abroad.

   I lift up my head . . .

MMP

17

The Big Questions (Cana)

"We did this earlier, traipsing to the well
over and over, so they could wash their precious feet.
Why again? What's the point? I thought
the problem was about wine!
Now, the sun's high, and the well is a long way off
I'd sooner be back drinking the stuff we took for
  ourselves."

"OK, OK, so you got the water. Now what?
I can't believe he said 'Take it to the M.C.!' – he
Is hardly so drunk as to think it's wine.
What is he about? Why does he want us to do it?"

"Ah! More wine at last – let's see – mmm . . .
That's the best yet. Great stuff! Rich, mouth-filling
taste, wonderful blackberry fruit, plenty of tannins.
Heavenly!
Why did they keep this till now?"

"I guess I needed that.
I didn't really want to start this so soon
but I suppose you have helped me, mother.
Why did you ask me just now, with that
look in your eye, as if you really knew?"

I saw all of this as it happened.
So many questions, puzzled faces
turning to open-eyed surprise and pleasure.
Then I knew the questions were wrong,
the wrong question. No-one could have
said why they did what they did
except 'He said to do it'.

I heard what he said, saw what he did
and went to him with other questions
What do you want me to do?
Who do you want me to be?

And he said "Be with me".   *MMP 20 January 2001*

18

Candle

Too short for a nine month's burning,
long for a touch of the Spirit, enough;
Sign of the saint, homing to the heart
reaching to the world with out-flung flame
imaging with ignatian industry
candle, companion of deep-felt times
lamp for the search of darkened nooks,
things hidden under stout defensive stones,
and unacknowledged treasures.

Lighten my lying darkness, lamp
and lead me on to that great greater light
of which you are the imitation – God.   *MMP*

Ruby Wedding

'Her value is greater than rubies',
so the writer of Proverbs has said;
but moving from past into present
turns black and white text to rich red.

Her beauty lies deep in her heart,
though not unexpressed in her face;
she loves as she lives, with a power –
source of gentle and passionate grace.

Forty years of a marriage have given
her family time – to discover
her values, bring joy and delight
to the hearts of all those who love her.   *JS*

Edinburgh Science Festival

Check on the route
Plan for a hoot
Fill up the boot
Head for the show.

Making a windmill
Thinking of landfill
Jungle safari, till
Doors close at five.

Reckless adventure bot
Blood-curdling Dr Clot
Everything hit the spot
Inside the brain.

Wheels on the dummy
Unwrap the mummy
Fill up the tummy
In between times.

Back at the double
Enter a bubble
Without any trouble
Dig up T-Rex.

All sowing seeds
For meeting our needs
Opening up leads
Selling our science.

For that's all the rage
In our frenetic age;
What's next on the page?
God only knows!

JS April 2011, written for his grandchildren

The Challenge

I have seen Hell; He comes with trumpets and
with beauty and with beckoning joy.
Is it so bad, this self that is *my* self
that I should welcome him with lifting heart?

I have seen Hell; She comes with cultured pose
that so enamours and attracts,
full of rich promise and allure
that captures for a moment all my heart.

I have seen both, and lived the brief delight
and something similar to joy.
Then tasted the metallic stain of blood
and emptiness, and dark despair.

I have seen Love, who sits with open arms
and open face, and open breaking heart.

MMP   May 2008

Buddleja Davidii

Buddleja davidii:
a Sunday name,
that such a kid as I
could share the fame
of Père David,
who truly came
to change a weed
like me, without an aim,
into a bush
for butterflies to claim.

*JS   Written at St Francis House, Hemingford Grey – Père
David was a famous missionary and botanist (acer davidii,
viburnum davidii etc); the poet is speaking as the buddleya
plant, which grows like a weed in spite of its posh name*

21

Waiting . . .

Waiting . . . all three of them,
waiting at the table,
order given, patiently
waiting . . .

a family, it seems,
father, son and daughter
fulfilling a promise given
waiting . . .

Waiting on . . . we have their order
simple to collect
ready, provided,
take it to the table

we have the privilege
of serving them today,
believing that they must
fulfil their promise

and so we wait on them.

Waiting . . . all three of them
father, son and daughter
sitting at the table
service given, order brought
meal delivered, wishing them
enjoyment . . .

Then suddenly the daughter rises from the table,
Her eyes compelling as a lambent flame,
Opens her arms in joy, until we see
that all are welcome at the feast who wait,
orphans and parents, young and old,
family members and the solitary ones;
there is enough for all, and all can eat,
fruits of the earth and work of human hands
the blessing of the Father, Son and Spirit.

MMP

Baptism

You - we - and special Three
becoming five or six? No,
more like one,
the Father's Son,
who with us all makes family:
it's five or six to one - just so.

JS   At Baptism there may be one or two parents present

The Wounds of Heaven

What wounds? Where? Why? How come?
Is he not Christ to joy and purpose bent?
Should we not grasp the proffered prize
with the slick fingers of enthusiasm?
Take! And regret! The wounds have said
his purposes are greater yet
and fuller still of joy and love
with healing power from above.

So let me dance in joyous play,
 I will delight to have my day.

MMP   25th March 2009, during a Retreat at St Beuno's

The Weaned Soul

Ah! I have longed to keep you close,
protected – no, I fear, controlled.
Yet you must dare the dance divine
here at the Stillpoint of my life
until the glory of your play
shines with an inward ecstasy
to gladden grief
and heal the wounds of heaven.

MMP   18th March 2009, during a Retreat at St Beuno's

What Flowers?

What flowers have blossomed, and then turned to seed?
Near seventy years of undergrowth, so casual, full of weed,
yet graced by sowing from a hand so sure
that one such seed, with all of life's manure
might clear a space for God to do his work,
to find his image, clean it for Christ's kirk.
God tends his man or woman, helps us cope
with all the mess of earth, and wait in hope.

What flowers will blossom in this time for me
that's left, to grow a bit, and learn to be?
Who knows when God will close the book
of life? So here and now I take a look
at what still buds within my mind and heart
and might, with God, just play its part
before death's sickle cuts us down to size.
A wreath? Far more – what's dead will rise.

JS   Written at the end of a Retreat at Hemingford Grey,
July09

Steeple and People

River of life, ending all strife,
Flowing from Christ who is temple and priest;
Wash down our streets, cleanse our conceits,
Open our jails and get us released
From under the steeple, to serving the people.

Spirit of life, cut out like a knife
Clutter and habits whose logic has ceased;
Pull up the blinds, broaden our minds,
Help us to serve a contemporary feast,
Not locked in the steeple, but meeting the people.

*JS   Written for a South Edinburgh Churches
Together event, 2010*

Saints in Concert

A concert of saints? Yes, really so:
gospel, reggae, jazz . . . and silence
under the baton of our maestro,
him who makes his presence
felt: God all the way down,
tumbling, touching, tasting death.
(Jesus is Lord.) Saints, lay down
your instruments, hold your breath
as arms that reach from God inside
are pinned to wood: God's elbow room
all gone, in flesh which really died
and lay unsung in Joseph's tomb
to wait, while hope pierced gates of hell
and time turned round within its track
so all things might at last be well.
It's gospel: Jesus Christ is back!

How shall we praise? Yes, still we ask
what style of music, rhythm, key?
We mess about . . . until we ask
just who is he – and who are we?

*JS Based on Philippians 2.6–11 and inspired by a talk
on the message of Hebrews given by Jeremy Begbie at a
Music and Worship Foundation event on 14th May 2011*

God, is there Room?

God, is there room in your life? Real room:
stuff we can talk about, like space and time,
spectacles, sparrows, even wheelbarrows?
Or had we better stick to sober topics:
truth and goodness, light and darkness . . .
Darkness!   What a staggered thing,
it holds our minds in sacred gloom
with Moses deep inside a rocky cleft
(for who can see the face of God and live?)
Darkness deep and dazzling: hidden optics
make god sense of each black whole,
shroud our hearts in holy mystery, and
weave new physics in that inner room.

JS   At a CARM Retreat, Glastonbury July 2011

Behind the Door

Is there anybody there?
A question haunting shrill debate
and quiet thought alike. Despair
and doubt may juggle balls of hope
and let them drop: that's fair
game for sceptics, but for patient
God a chance to show his flair
for search and dusty enterprise
within our broken faith: repair
it, bring all damaged things together
in one man, for everyone to wear
his faith, his hope, new birthday suit
for me, for you, for all who dare
to look behind the ivy-covered door.

*JS   Composed at a Quiet Day in January 2011, led by
the Lantern Group*

That Quiet Day in Haddington featured an ivy-covered door placed to look rather like the door in Holman Hunt's painting, which was based in turn on Revelation 3.20

Contents